Early Americans

by Stephanie Sigue

Editorial Offices: Glenview, Illinois • Parsippany, New Jersey • New York, New York

Sales Offices: Needham, Massachusetts • Duluth, Georgia • Glenview, Illinois
Coppell, Texas • Sacramento, California • Mesa, Arizona

American Indians is a term that is used to describe the first people who lived in this land. You may have heard of the Navajo, the Apache, the Cheyenne, and the Sioux. These are well-known American Indian groups. The Chumash lived in California. Their **culture** played a major role in the settling of early California.

American Indian Names

Many places in the United States have American Indian names. You may have heard the names *Massachusetts, Delaware,* and *Huron.* These are the names of two states and a Great Lake. All three of these names are of American Indian origin.

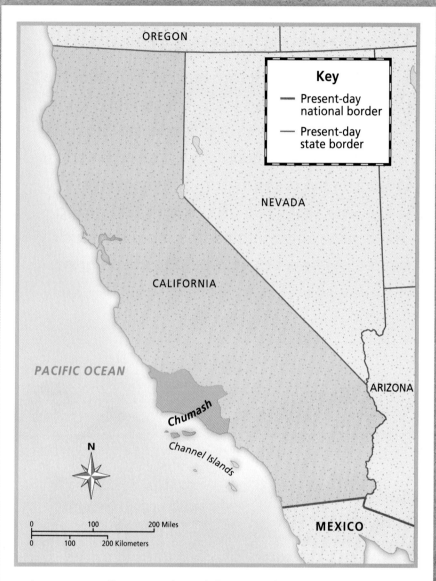

OREGON

NEVADA

CALIFORNIA

PACIFIC OCEAN

Chumash

Channel Islands

ARIZONA

MEXICO

N

Key

— Present-day
national border

— Present-day
state border

0   100   200 Miles
0   100   200 Kilometers

This map of coastal California shows where the
Chumash lived.

The Early Chumash

Before the Spanish arrived in California, the Chumash lived along the south central coast of California. They lived in a connected group of villages. They had contact with other American Indians in the western part of the country.

The very first Chumash villages had only a few houses and contained no more than sixty people. As time passed, the population grew.

A Village Chief

Each village had a chief. The Chumash had a class system, and the title of chief was **hereditary**. It was passed down from a parent to a child.

A chief was expected to be honest, strong, good at hunting and fishing, and able to get along with people. The chief often had to settle arguments. As the villages became larger, it was sometimes necessary for a chief to declare war.

What the Chumash Ate

The Chumash ate meat, fish, and wild plant parts. Oak trees provided the Chumash with acorns. All of the plant parts used by the Chumash for food were gathered, not grown. The Chumash were not farmers.

After they gathered the acorns, Chumash women would grind the nuts into flour. Acorn flour was used to make different types of food, such as breadlike loaves.

The Chumash had uses for other plants. They dug up a plant called *soaproot*. They used it as a shampoo and for washing their skin and clothing. They also made brushes out of it. These brushes could be used as tools for preparing food or for cave painting. Best of all, they ate it. After being roasted in an oven the bulbs made delicious treats.

The Chumash had uses for every part of a plant. They knew what to do with the flowers, stems, leaves, seeds, roots, and bulbs.

Chumash Boats

The Chumash lived on the mainland and on the Channel Islands. They needed a way to go back and forth between the mainland and the islands.

The Chumash built plank canoes called *tomols.* The boat was made from planks cut from driftwood. The planks were sewn together. Then the joints were sealed with pitch, or tar. After the canoes were finished, they were painted red and decorated with seashells.

Fishing and Hunting

Most Chumash men were fishermen. Sometimes they fished from their canoes with a hook and line. Other times they used fish traps, spears, clubs, and nets to catch fish.

The Chumash hunted animals such as deer, elk, antelope, rabbits, and squirrels. The Chumash were very quiet hunters. Wearing animal skins often helped Chumash hunters to close in on their prey without being noticed.

Ceremonies and Fiestas

The Chumash loved celebrations. The winter solstice, or the shortest day of the year, was the most important celebration.

Three people had special duties at Chumash celebrations. They were the chief, the *shaman,* or religious leader, and the *paxa.* One of the chief's main duties was to make sure that there was enough food. The *paxa* was in charge of the festival. The *paxa* chose the **site** for the special dances. He made sure that everything went smoothly.

Chumash Cave Paintings

A shaman was a religious leader. This can be seen in the rock paintings that have been found in mountain caves. Because of the paintings' locations, many believe that only a shaman was allowed in the caves.

The Chumash cave paintings have many different patterns. One Chumash painting shows a ship. Others look like figures based on heavenly bodies.

This is an example of a Chumash cave painting.

Baskets and Tools

The Chumash made some of the finest baskets ever created. The baskets were made using plants similar to tall reeds. The Chumash wove designs into the fibers. These baskets have lasted for centuries and can be seen in many museums.

The Chumash made interesting tools. They made knives, scrapers, and arrowheads by grinding and sharpening different types of stone. Fishing hooks were made from the shells of clams and other shellfish.

Chumash artisans, or skilled workers, carved wood to make bowls and musical instruments.

These are examples of Chumash rattles.

The Chumash and the Missions

In the mid-1700s the Spanish began building **missions** in California. This event marked the end of the Chumash way of life.

The **missionaries** captured many Chumash and forced them to work at the missions. Poor food, bad treatment, and disease killed thousands. Many Chumash revolted, but they could not escape.

The Decline of the Chumash

In 1775, as the missionaries were just beginning to arrive, the Chumash population was about 22,000. In 1885, 100 years later, only eighty-four remained. By 1906 only forty-two were still alive.

The Chumash lands became part of a United States territory in 1848. The Chumash continued to suffer. By the early 1900s there were very few Chumash left. By the 1970s there were no fluent speakers of the Chumash language alive.

Today 287 Chumash live on the small Santa Ynez Reservation in California. About 2,000 people claim Chumash ancestry.

Glossary

culture the way of life of a particular people including customs, religion, ideas, inventions, and tools

hereditary passed down from parents to children

mission a settlement set up to teach religion

missionary a person sent by a religious group to spread its religion

site a place where something is located

Early Americans

by Stephanie Sigue

PEARSON
Scott
Foresman

Editorial Offices: Glenview, Illinois • Parsippany, New Jersey • New York, New York

Sales Offices: Needham, Massachusetts • Duluth, Georgia • Glenview, Illinois
Coppell, Texas • Sacramento, California • Mesa, Arizona